I0004673

Intruders at the Gate!

Building an Effective
Malware Defense System

Jeff Hoffman

Intruders at the Gate -
Building an effective Malware Defense System

ISBN:1500479578
ISBN-13:9781500479572

DEDICATION

This book is dedicated to my wife and best friend Deborah
who makes getting up each morning so worthwhile.

Intruders at the Gate -
Building an effective Malware Defense System

Intruders at the Gate -
Building An Effective Malware Defense System

Intruders at the Gate -
Building an effective Malware Defense System

CONTENTS

Intruders at the Gate -
Building an effective Malware Defense System

Who This Book Is Intended To Help

I've written this book to provide guidance to small and mid-sized businesses on how to improve their defenses against the ever increasing threat of malware. Building an effective defense mechanism for your network takes time and patience. Gone are the days when adding an anti-virus program to your computers was all it took to keep your business safe.

Today's business environment dictates that your network be connected if not fully integrated with the public Internet and as such the avenues open to hackers and other intruders have expanded greatly. You must be prepared to deal with the consequences of that integration. Your employees connect to the Internet almost constantly in many ways via e-mail, browsing, social media, personal devices and outbound worker connectivity. The number of employees who work at least a portion of the work week outside of the office has increased by over 70% in the last decade. All of these interactions with the Internet have created a significant increase in vulnerable entry points into your network. Larger organizations with in-house IT staffs can dedicate technicians to securing company IT resources and still the bad guys find ways to steal or corrupt data. Smaller organizations don't have the luxury of full-time, skilled security experts to protect their networks and that's why I've created this book. Hopefully, it will demonstrate ways to protect your most valuable business resource – your data.

The Goals of this Book

Perhaps the most serious threat facing business automation today is the ever increasing threat of data loss by malware infections, neglect or outright theft. Let's take a second to look at the various threats your business faces. If you mention the word "Disaster", the first thing most business people think of is physical loss, IE. "What happens if my business is physically damaged or destroyed?" Of course, that's a legitimate concern but let's face it, that's what insurance is for. My point is that the data that makes up the underpinnings of your business is its most valuable asset. Insurance will replace a lost computer, a destroyed building or other asset but it can't easily rebuild or replace lost data. It may not pay for a lost accounts receivables data base. Your data assets are your most fragile and most difficult to replace asset.

On a possibly more important level, insurance can't repair your business reputation if you lose someone else's confidential data. Your credibility as a well-run business can be seriously jeopardized when word gets out that you lost confidential information belonging to someone else. You can also be held liable as new laws are holding victims of hacking responsible for the consequences of neglectful data protection practices.

We're going to show you what you're up against, how you can be vulnerable via different intrusion mechanisms and how you can take steps to forestall the inevitable exploits that will attack your business network. There's an adage in IT security circles that states "It's not a matter of IF you're going to be hacked, it's just a matter of WHEN." If I may be so bold to add, "It's all a matter of how well you're prepared when it happens and how you react."

That's what this book is about. My goal is to help you understand what you're really up against and show you some better ways to protect yourself.

The 8 Key Points of Network Vulnerability

In the diagram below, I've identified the 8 key vulnerability points for any network regardless of size. These are the places where malware and intrusions can enter your network and the areas you have to understand and protect. Please recognize, of course, that there are many sub categories that could be broken out but for this discussion, we'll deal with these broad categories.

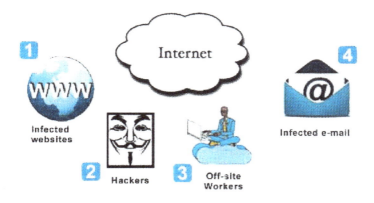

8 Critical Points of Vulnerability

Vulnerability #1

Infected web sites have become one of the most popular ways to deliver malware to computers. Statistically, web delivered malware has overtaken e-mail as the #1 delivery method used by hackers to infect computers and networks. They take advantage of out-of-date browsers, programs (also called apps), utilities and operating systems to embed content on vulnerable PC's which in turn can infect and damage servers. A significant percentage of malware is delivered via legitimate but infected web sites. We'll talk more about this in greater depth in subsequent chapters.

Vulnerability #2

Hackers are a constant threat to insufficiently protected network connections. These are the "Direct Threat" risks because they attack your network directly either through your Internet connection or other open connections. Very frequently, a web or e-mail delivered malware will open communication with a hacker command-and-control-server that allows further direct exploitation of your network.

Vulnerability #3

Off-premises workers can also become a threat unwittingly because their computers may be a source of infection either through pass-through infections or improperly maintained security settings outside of your control. If you don't exercise control of ALL remote devices that connect to your network this can be a big risk exposure point for your network. Here's a perfect example: employee A likes to do "extra" work from home using his own PC. While browsing the Internet, his son visits a site that infects his PC with a keylogger malware. When employee accesses the company network from home using the now-infected home PC, the keylogger tracks and captures his login information to the company system. That information is then reported to a remote command-and-control server operated by the hacker who now knows everything needed to exploit the company network using information unwittingly provided by employee A.

Vulnerability #4

Probably the biggest threat to your network is malware and social engineering threats delivered by e-mail. Practically all employees have e-mail either through your domain or through a personal account on a public e-mail service. Without proper control of this entry point, you are leaving a hole in your network security a mile wide! In this vulnerability category we're also going to lump in IM (Instant Messaging) activity which can also be a point of Intrusion. We'll talk about this in greater detail later on.

Vulnerability #5

Never discount the threat from disgruntled employees both current and former. Resist the urge to think "Oh, my people would never do that!" You'd be surprised at the regularity with which businesses fall victim to in-house threats! Robert Sullivan of MSNBC reported in May, 2014 that Michigan State professor Judith Collins has discovered that perhaps as much as 70 percent of all identity theft originates with company employees.

Vulnerability #6

Improperly configured Wi-Fi connections are a real threat. Wireless isn't as secure as many people think and because it isn't constrained physically like a wired network, your network vulnerability is extended beyond the physical limits of your office. I'll share some stories with you later about this. By not controlling this aspect of your perimeter, infected computers can gain access to your network and expose it to all sorts of infections. Hackers can "sniff" your network via any poorly configured access points and find a weak point in your defenses through which they can insert their malware.

Vulnerability #7

The proliferation of portable media has greatly increased the "leak factor" for data theft. Do you know what data leaves your office every night at quitting time on flash drives? If left unchecked, your critical business secrets could be walking out the door undetected. The other side of the coin for portable media is what can be brought onto you network unwittingly by visitors and staff when malware piggybacks onto flash drives and when connected to a computer, infects your network and bypasses your perimeter defenses. In a 2009 study by the Ponemon Institute, they found that 59% of employees who quit or were asked to leave took confidential or sensitive business information with them when they left.

Vulnerability #8

BYOD is the buzzword that employees love and IT security specialists hate. The lack of control on portable employee devices coming onto and leaving your computer network creates a whole new level of exposure that has to be addressed and secured. You need to address the use of non-company computers on your network. There's a whole world of threats to consider lurking on those devices. Ignore this vulnerability at your own risk!

A Short History of Malware Infections

First, let's define what we're talking about when we discuss malware. People who don't deal with this stuff every day get confused by the term malware and how it differs from the more commonly used term virus. Essentially, malware is a broader definition of the same thing – unwanted programs that can harm your network or steal your information. I won't bore you with the technical delineations. Malware is a contraction of the words Malicious Software and includes computer viruses, ransomware, worms, Trojan horses, rootkits, keyloggers, dialers, spyware, adware, malicious BHOs, fake security software, and other malicious programs.

Malware can be delivered using a variety of techniques including e-mail, infected web sites, direct hacker infections, infected portable devices and media and even via Wi-Fi.

According to AV-Test Gmbh in 2013, over 85 million new malwares were detected by their labs while McAfee claimed they detected an average of over 100,000 new malwares each day last year for a total of about 36.5 million malwares. Kaspersky labs claimed they detected over 300,000 new malwares each day in 2012 or about 109.5 million for the year. No matter which total you believe, you've got to admit that they're all pretty staggering numbers!

Here's the basic problem. As competitors, Anti-Virus companies don't really talk to each other and share information. Each company does their own thing with their own staffs and come up with differing solutions to defeat the hackers that write all of this stuff.

According to a Ponemon Institute study in October, 2012, they determined that small organizations incur a significantly higher per capita cost than larger organizations ($1,324 versus $305) for cybercrime like hacking events, information theft and malware intrusions. Never think that you're too small to be a target for hackers. While the payday for hacking large organizations might be bigger, small organizations tend to be easier targets because they don't have the resources that bigger companies have to protect themselves.

To give you an idea of how fast your network can be compromised, consider two statistics experts provide on infection speeds and corresponding remediation times.

The amount of time between when a hacking attempt starts until a successful compromise is achieved is:

Within Seconds   - 11%
Within Minutes   - 13%
Within an Hour   - 60%
Longer   - 16%

Now consider, that once a network is compromised, the typical attacker goes undetected for 243 days according to Mandiant Corporation, a leading security management form.

84% of network intrusions are accomplished in under an hour and once a network is infected the average time it takes to figure it out is 243 days? YIKES!

You've got to admit those are some pretty scary statistics. For now, I'm just trying to give you a feel for the scope of the security threats you're facing every day.

How can you tell if your network has been compromised? Here are 10 of the most common symptoms:

1. Unexplained increase in administrative logons on your network during off-hours.
2. Increase in outbound connection activity to unknown outside servers/devices.
3. Discovery of back-door Trojans on PCs, endpoints or network shares.
4. Excessive or unusual network traffic.

5. Large unexplained data movement or additions of data within your network.
6. SSL-encrypted network traffic using methods not typically used in your organization.
7. Excessive Applications Event Log traffic including A/V or firewall start and stop commands.
8. A-typical slowness on your network or Internet connection.
9. Unusual Pop-up messages on network computers or servers.
10. Files that don't won't open because of no matching application.

And let's not forget the more obvious signs of infection like this:

Of course, there are many more possibilities but that's our Top 10 list of common symptoms.

What Motivates Malware Writers?

In a single word – Money! There's a lot of money to be made in a very short time if you're good at writing malware code. Malware authors can either use it themselves to exploit others or, easier yet, write the code and then either sell it or rent it to others and let them do the actual dirty work.

According to Dell Secureworks, in just the first 100 days after CryptoLocker was introduced into the wild in September, 2013, the authors raked in over $30 million.

In an article from CNN on June 3, 2014 entitled "Cybercrime is big money for hackers"   James Lewis reported "According to one European intelligence service, there are 20 to 30 criminal gangs in the former Soviet Union that have hacking skills as good as most nations. There are many other groups with lesser skills. These criminals are nimble and inventive, and there are thriving cybercrime black markets where you can buy the latest hacking tools. This means there are highly skilled criminals who live in safe havens but can use the Internet to commit crimes that can earn millions of dollars, for which they will never be arrested or tried. Why would they stop? While there is good cooperation among some Western countries against cybercrime, Russia has little interest in stopping these groups."

Speaking of cybercrime black markets, according to Mathew J. Schwartz in Information Week publication Dark Reading- "The gang behind the Blackhole crimeware toolkit has earned so much money from renting their malicious software that the creator has been given $100,000 to procure the best Web browser exploits and zero-day flaws" to make that tool even "better".   Blackhole can be rented on-line for as little as $50 per day or $1,500 per year so any hacker can use it to deliver their own payload.   The same gang also released a $10,000 per month exploit kit called the Cool Exploit in late 2012. There are dozens if not hundreds of other kits available on-line that perform similar tasks for a fee.

A pretty well known Black Hat hacker explained the process of running his 3 million PC botnet, which he calls "The Black Shadow Project". Clients pay for his services, like 1 million spam messages sent in 50,000 piece blocks for $150, as well as performing DDoS attacks on their targets of choice. He also claims that he sends out 90 million spam emails a day to "anyone and everyone." If you do the math, $150 per million spams times 90 million per day equals $13,500 per day. I'll bet you didn't think that spam was worth that much money. AND he's just one of hundreds doing this every day!

This hacker says that he only accepts BitCoin and other electronic coinage which he later converts into US dollars, an anonymous way to launder money and fund his operation.

How much does he make and does he fear getting caught? He replied "I can make $15-20K in an hour. Jail doesn't concern me."

The essential problem is that the Internet is an international platform and there presently aren't many cross-border laws that apply. What's illegal in the U.S. probably isn't legal in Eastern Europe or Russia. That makes enforcement almost impossible. Sure, occasionally the Secret Service or the FBI may catch a foreign hacker if he or she makes the mistake of entering the U.S. but for the most part, these people know where to set up shop with the least risk of prosecution.

Types of Malware and their Entry Points

First, let's talk a little about the types of attacks and their efficiency historically. In Table #1, Ponemon Research studied 56 organizations and tallied how many of those companies had experienced the various categories of malware related intrusion. As you can see, every organization had been attacked via Viruses, Worms or Trojans and almost 3 out of 4 had been victimized by a Botnet attack. With the exception of the category Stolen Devices, all of the others attack vectors shown are in some way related to the various types of Malware.

Table #1 Types of Intrusions/Cyber Attacks experienced by 56 benchmarked companies	
Viruses, Worms, Trojans	100%
Other Malware	96%
Botnets	71%
Web-based Attacks	64%
Stolen Devices	46%
Malicious Code	38%
Malicious Insiders	38%
Phone and Social Engineering	38%
Denial of Service Attack	32%
Source: Ponemon Study – Cost of Cyber-Crime, October, 2012	

Keep in mind that Malware is not a single "thing" but a broad category of malicious programs designed to extract information or money from your employees and/or organization.

Some of the more commonly known types of malware are viruses, worms, Trojans, bots, back doors, spyware, ransomware and adware. Damage from malware varies from causing minor irritation (such as browser popup ads), to stealing confidential information or money, destroying data, and compromising and/or entirely disabling systems and networks. Here are short definitions of some of the most common types of malware and what they do.

Viruses

A computer virus is a type of malware that propagates by inserting a copy of itself into and becoming part of another program. It spreads from one computer to another, leaving infections as it travels. Viruses can range in severity from causing mildly annoying effects to damaging data or software and causing denial-of-service

(DoS) conditions. Almost all viruses are attached to an executable file, which means the virus may exist on a system but will not be active or able to spread until a user runs or opens the malicious host file or program.

Worms

Practically speaking, a worm is an evolved form of a virus. Like a virus, worms too replicate and spread themselves but it happens on a bit larger scale. Also, unlike a virus, a worm does not need a human action to replicate and spread and that's what makes it more dangerous. A worm always searches for network loopholes to replicate from computer to computer and thus most common methods of computer intrusion are emails and IM attachments.

Trojans

A Trojan is named after the wooden horse the Athenians used to infiltrate Troy – an apparent gift that turns nasty once inside your defenses. It is a harmful piece of software that looks legitimate but isn't. Users are typically tricked into loading and executing it on their systems. After it is activated, it can achieve any number of attacks on the host, from irritating the user (popping up windows or changing desktop settings) to damaging the host (deleting files, stealing data, or activating and spreading other malware, such as viruses). Trojans are also known to create back doors to give hackers access to your system or reporting to another command-and-control-center to await new instructions.

Unlike viruses and worms, Trojans do not reproduce by infecting other files nor do they self-replicate. Trojans most often spread through user interaction such as opening an e-mail attachment or downloading, running a file from the Internet and even Instant Messaging (IM) conversations.

Spyware

Spywares are also malicious programs that can be installed on computers but unlike any of the above they don't intend to harm your computer. Instead, they spy on you. Once installed, they run in the background and collect your personal data. These can include your credit card numbers, passwords, important files and many other pieces of personal information. Spywares can track your keystrokes, scan and read your computer files, snoop IM chats and emails and heaven knows what else. Users who complain about their computer running slow are most often the victims of multiple instances of spyware clogging up their PC resources collecting stuff. So-called Freeware programs that are downloaded by employees are some of the most common sources of Spyware as are free toolbars that attach to your browser.

Rootkit

Rootkits are what I refer to as "Malware – The Next Generation". While technically not a new phenomenon, they have grown in complexity and have become much more widespread. Unlike simple viruses or worms, they are designed by attackers to gain root or administrative access to your computer and bury themselves deeper into the operating system to hide better and are much more difficult to remove. Once an attacker gains admin privilege, it becomes a cakewalk for him to exploit your system. Because they're more deeply insinuated into the operating system, they are much more effective at hiding from or defeating anti-virus or anti-malware programs.

Bots

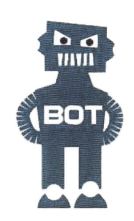

"Bot" is derived from the word "robot" and is an automated process that interacts with other network services or off-network devices. Bots often automate tasks and provide information or services that would otherwise be conducted by a human being. Bots can be used for either good or malicious intent. A malicious bot is self-propagating malware designed to infect a host and connect back to a central server that acts as a command and control (C&C) center for an entire network of compromised devices, or "botnet." With a botnet, attackers can launch broad-based, "remote-control," flood-type attacks against their target(s). In addition to the worm-like ability to self-propagate, bots can include the ability to log keystrokes, gather passwords, capture and analyze packets, gather financial information, launch DoS attacks, relay spam, and open back doors on infected computers.

Bots have all the advantages of worms, but are generally much more versatile in their infection techniques and are often modified within hours of publication to alter their identity. They have been known to exploit back doors opened by worms and viruses, which allows them to access networks that have good perimeter control. Bots rarely announce their presence, instead they infect networks in a way that escapes immediate notice.

BotNets are used frequently in Denial of Service (DDoS or DoS) Attacks.

RATS

RAT stands for Remote Administrative Tool and while some of them are legitimate tools, in this context, they are not. Typically delivered by Trojans and other malware delivery systems, these are similar to Backdoors but typically are controlled by Command and Control servers for keylogging, DoS and other data theft purposes. These may stay memory resident in systems and are re-initiated by rogue entries in the Registry of your system.

Denial of Service (DoS)

Denial of Service Attacks (DoS)

Target "Many Against One"

Political "hacktivists" frequently use this technique against government or financial sites to bury the network connection of their target in traffic to drive them off-line as a form of protest. Sometimes regular businesses can become victims of this type of exploit. Denial of service attacks are intended to occupy all of the capacity of the intended target by flooding it with traffic to overwhelm its bandwidth capacity or its defense systems ability to respond or do anything else productive during the attack. They do this by using "Zombie" computers to participate in the attack under the control of a Command and Control server.

The Denial of Service attack occurs when dozens, hundreds or even thousands of Bot-infected computers (Zombies) receive instructions from a Command and Control Server to all target a single location and pound it with traffic to overwhelm the target with electronic traffic beyond its ability to respond and force it to fail either driving it off-line or possibly by failing in a way that opens a crack in your defenses to exploit your network.

Ransomware

Ransomware

I've got your network! PAY UP!

As the name implies, the goal of ransomware is to extort payment to undo damage that the program does to your system or network. Of the many instances of ransomware out there, one of the most well-known was Crypto-Locker. It loads onto a computer either via an e-mail attachment or through an infected web site. It runs in memory first so anti-virus programs won't detect it and begins encrypting every file that it can access including network shares using very high level encryption methods which makes all of those files useless. It then displays a message demanding payment for the decryption key to unscramble the file. If you're not properly prepared, this malware is a very tricky and expensive problem to clean up.

Back Doors

Backdoor Exploits

Although technically not considered malware themselves, Back Doors are a significant vulnerability for computers or networks and are usually a byproduct of a successful malware intrusion. A back door is an undocumented way of accessing a system bypassing normal authentication mechanisms. Some back doors are placed in software by the original programmer and others are placed on systems through a system compromise, such as a virus or worm. Usually, attackers use back doors for easier and continued access to a system after it has been compromised.

Brute Force Attacks

Brute force attacks are essentially concentrated attempts to force an opening in your network by sheer volume of port scans looking for openings or dictionary attacks to guess passwords on your network. Using easy-to-guess or common passwords are what typically allows this type of intrusion to work. The word password and 123456 are such commonly used passwords on networks it's almost embarrassing! The key to the success of Brute Force attacks is persistence. In layman's terms, if they persist in their attack long enough and you allow it to go on, it's only a matter of time before they'll get in. Almost every Internet connection in the world has experienced a Brute Force attack and odds are most of them went undetected because so few networks even bother to look for them.

Traditional Malware Defenses

You're probably asking yourself "Why doesn't my anti-virus program catch all of this junk?" That's a reasonable question. In this section, I'll show you how anti-virus programs attempt to stop the tidal wave of malware being generated each day.

Traditional malware and network defense has been a two layered process. You installed a firewall at your networks entry point that was intended to regulate traffic going in and out of your Internet connection and to manage communication with off-site locations with the goal of keeping "the bad guys" aka Hackers out of your network. Then you installed an anti-virus program on your local computers to remove viruses using signature-based detection and you had. That was about the extent of traditional anti-malware defense.

Firewalls

Traditional Malware Defense

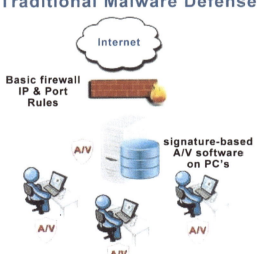

Originally, firewalls were designed to manage traffic on your network and to provide IP address-based and Port-based access limitations. What are those? Every place on the Internet is identified by an IP address so if you wanted to keep someone out, you set an IP rule dictating who could get in or who to keep out. As far as ports, without getting too technical, each type of communication traffic on the Internet uses a special port. For example, www traffic uses port #80 and e-mail traffic uses several ports like 25 or 110. Port #443 is used for secure web traffic (HTTPS).

There are virtually thousands of port numbers that can be used on the Internet so to keep unwanted traffic out of a network, IT security staffs will establish port-based rules in the firewall. At the most basic level "Let traffic on this port in, Keep traffic on that port out!" is essentially how it worked. That worked fine for years until hackers stated using legitimate ports for their own purposes. Suddenly, port 80, which in the past wasn't considered much of a threat, became a vehicle of various types of intrusion tactics and because all web users were dependent upon that port IT people couldn't just shut it down with a port rule. Web (WWW) traffic was no longer totally safe. Something more was needed at the perimeter to keep your network safe and traditional methods no longer worked. The same became true as Hackers became more adept at corrupting previously "safe" Internet ports with their exploits.

Traditional Signature-based Anti-Virus
Simple signature-based anti-virus techniques also became overwhelmed with the tidal wave of new and constantly changing virus signatures. As recently as 8 years ago, the amount of malware generated worldwide was reasonably manageable. In 2006, for example, the total number of malwares generated worldwide was about 180,000 or about 490 instances per day. By 2012, that annual malware volume was being generated in a single hour on the Internet. As you can imagine, keeping up with that tidal wave became nearly impossible. Response times for malware remediation began to skyrocket.

The anti-virus companies claim some pretty big numbers of detected malware but the key question that has to be asked is "How fast do they catch them?" The key to malware containment is response time. For example, the Romans claimed to have stopped Attila the Hun in the year 453 AD but not before he laid waste to most of Europe for about 20 years. Yes, he was stopped so I suppose they could claim victory but how much damage was done before they finally got it done? IT security works best in the here and now. How fast you react means everything in anti-malware security. Waiting even a day for a solution can mean incurring devastating damage to your business network.

Hackers and malware authors learned years ago that sheer volume can overwhelm the anti-virus publishers and the current competitive marketplace for A/V software further complicates the matter.

Why Traditional A/V Doesn't Work Anymore

Let's examine today's reality in the world of malware fighting. One of the top anti-virus companies in the world claims to have a lab with 200 detection specialists working on malware detection and remediation. Take that 180,000 per hour new malware generated figure we talked about earlier and lets' do the math. If every one of those 200 specialists worked every hour of every day, they still would have to detect, diagnose and neutralize 900 malwares every hour. That's 15 resolutions needed every minute of every day just to keep up! Sadly no one can work that hard for that long! You get the picture?

Let's talk about the way most anti-virus programs have worked for a second.

A-V protection is a multi-stage process:

1. First someone has to detect the malware in the wild (out there on the Internet). There are currently over 2.4 billion computers out there worldwide and first someone has to report it to an A/V Company as a problem.

2. The A/V Company traps the detected malware and reverse engineers the code in it to discover its unique coding characteristic called "The Signature".

3. The third step is to develop a counter measure to stop or remove it.

4. The A/V Company then publishes an update the new "Signature" and the appropriate counter measure to their signature file data base for their clients and wait for them to download the update to their computers.

5. Finally, your version of their product on your computer or network is updated either manually or via an automated process and THEN you're ready to detect and remove the new malware.

Each anti-virus vendor has their own detection labs staff with dozens or sometimes hundreds of techs tasked with finding and neutralizing malware each day. Back in 2006, it was a lot easier to keep up with 400-500 malware generated per day.

As the volume of malware has grown exponentially in the last few years, can you get an appreciation for the difficulty of keeping your defenses up-to-date?

And that's not all! Read on for more bad news on the malware defenses front lines!

Malware Morphing and Changing Signatures

Now imagine that Hackers invented a way to make Signature-based malware protection obsolete. Morphing malware seeks to defeat traditional anti-virus software by changing its "signature" look because that's the method that A/V software relies upon to detect malware. The ability to constantly change its look or signature keeps malware one step ahead of the A/V good guys. The process of changing malware signatures on the fly is referred to as Polymorphic Malware or "Morphing Malware" for short. There have even been some reports of malware that changes its characteristic signature every few installations, making previous A/V signature files useless finding new instances of the same malware.

Imagine, if you will, how much harder the FBI's job would be if everyone on their Top 10 Most Wanted list could change their appearance before the printer could even create a wanted poster to distribute to all the local police departments. Now imagine trying to keep up with millions of malware signatures worldwide.

Remember what I said earlier, each of the many A-V companies does its own thing. They don't always talk to one another. Just because Trend-Micro A/V detected a malware doesn't mean that McAfee did too at the same moment. As competitors, they don't share their discoveries with each other. There are a couple of dozen anti-virus and anti-malware companies out there. Some have bigger labs than others and some programs are better than others so results vary from one vendor to the next. We'll talk more about that in the chapter entitled "Which Products Work Best?"

. . . and then came Advanced Volatile Threats!

The fight between hackers and security experts is a real cat and mouse game and these mice are VERY smart. Most anti-virus programs are designed to look for malware as it is written to your hard drive. What if the bad guys figured out how to avoid that process? If a particular malware could stay memory resident and never attempted a write to the hard drive while the A/V program is only inspecting data written to the hard drive it could go a long time without being detected, right? Well, they did it!

A recent phenomenon that makes malware detection an even bigger nightmare is Advanced Volatile Threats or AVT's for short (we IT guys love our acronyms!) These guys are different in that they never infect your hard drive. Remember when I said that almost all traditional anti-virus programs look for infections as they write to your hard drives. These guys stop just short of that and instead stay in memory to do their business to escape detection. Advanced Volatile Threats (AVT) are an advanced kind of cyber-attack where the malicious code does not need to reach its victim's hard drive in order to deliver its payload. They take advantage of flaws in memory resident apps or programs such as Java to fulfill their mission. Now A/V vendors have another hole in the dike to plug.

Enter Heuristic Virus/Malware Detection

Newer versions of Anti-virus software may use one or several "heuristic" techniques to proactively detect malware in addition to their signature-based detection methods. The main essence of each of these methods is to analyze the suspicious file's characteristics and behavior to determine if it is indeed malware before you let it through your defenses. Here are a few of the common heuristic/behavioral scanning techniques:

Malware Sandboxing

File Emulation: Also known as "sandbox testing" or dynamic scanning, file emulation allows a suspicious file to run in a controlled virtual system (or "sandbox") to see what it does. Think of this approach as watching the virus in a sterile testing room with a two-way mirror. If the file acts like a virus even if it doesn't show up in the signature file list, it's deemed a virus and not allowed onto the network.

File Analysis: File analysis involves the software taking an in-depth look at the file and trying to determine its intent, destination, and purpose. Perhaps the file has instructions to delete certain files or

Intruders at the Gate

is trying to establish communication with another un-trusted server on the Internet, and should be considered a virus.

The problem here is the risk of false positives impeding the processes of legitimate software because it's not always a precise method of detection. These extra inspection steps can also add overhead to your computer or network. Each vendor's heuristic techniques are different as you'd expect and some are better than others.

How effective is Malware Sandboxing?

The key problem with Heuristic A/V detection is false positives. That's where the A/V diagnoses a legitimate process or program as malware and stops it from running, or worse, deletes it. To paraphrase an old adage, just because it walks like a duck, and quacks like a duck doesn't mean it's always a duck!

Heuristic Malware detection does require a good deal of tweaking, tuning and maintenance. At this point in its life-cycle, it's still not a fool-proof technology but it's getting better.

So who's the best A/V Company?

First let me say that the answer to that question changes frequently as each of the major players updates their product. There are several good research and rating systems that grade companies in this segment of the market and while individual rankings may change a little from year to year, I believe it's safe to say that there are about 5 key market leaders that consistently outperform the rest of the pack. Gartner Research is one of the leading research organizations in the IT industry. Below is their ranking chart for A/V products for 2014.

If you're using Gartner Research as your rankings bible, when reading Gartner's "Magic Quadrant" please understand that they rank vendors by how well their processes are designed to work and how well they execute that design.

Essentially most Gartner (an others) product evaluations group players in a given product group them like this by the completeness of their vision and their ability to execute on that vision. There are normally 4 rankings or classifications:

Industry Rankings for EndPoint Protection (A/V)	
Rankings	**Companies**
Industry Leaders	Symantec, McAfee Trend Micro Kaspersky Sophos
Challengers	Microsoft
Visionaries	Panda Webroot IBM Landesk Luminension Security Arkoon
Niche Players	Eset Bitdefender F-Secure Check Point Security Technologies and a couple of other less well-known names
Source: Gartner Magic Quadrant for Endpoint protection platforms 2014	

What does each ranking mean: Essentially, as you'd expect from the ranking Industry Leaders they offer a well thought out and complete product and can deliver good results with that product.

Testing indicated that Challengers perform what they do pretty well but their product may not be as comprehensive or complete as an Industry Leader.

Visionaries is a nice way of identifying a product that has a complete offering but it wasn't necessarily as effective as the first 2 categories during the evaluation.

Niche players don't offer a complete solution and don't necessarily perform very well in the tests the evaluator put the product through. That could be because the product wasn't designed as a total protection device or it just performed poorly in the overall testing.

Are you using a product not listed in the rankings? Maybe you're using a consumer rated product instead of a commercial product OR just maybe you're using a product that failed to measure up to commercial grade standards.

Most of the professional research organizations express similar opinions. Why stop at the Top 5 vendors? Frankly, after the top 5, there's a pretty big gap between them and the rest of the pack in the world of A/V software. Are the others worthless? No, let's just say that these 5 are the leaders.

Before you run out and buy the Symantec product and scrap your Sophos A/V based upon the Gartner Magic Quadrant, I'd like to remind you that these 5 companies consistently jockey with each other and the differences in performance are probably negligible in a practical sense. The technical differences that Gartner used to differentiate them may not be relevant to your particular situation. There are a lot more things that go into these ratings than simple A/V efficiency. In a general sense, you can consider all 5 of these companies the winners just for making it into the "Leaders" rankings. The key is to stick with a company that consistently appears as a leader in A/V category. If your current A/V solutions doesn't appear at all on the rankings, you've got your work cut out for yourself finding a new A/V product.

For Heaven's sake, avoid using those so-called "Free" anti-virus products! There are several on the market. I personally believe in the old adage "You get what you pay for." Is your business worth so little that you'd risk it to a product that the author doesn't think enough of to charge a fee for it?

Differentiating Anti-Virus From Anti-Malware Programs

At their essence, the two types of programs are quite different. Most anti-virus programs are designed to keep viruses and malware from getting onto your hard drive. Anti-Malware programs, on the other hand, mostly focus on removing those types of software once they are already on your hard drive. Yes, there is a little cross-over but generally that's the difference.

As I've pointed out earlier, both products rely heavily on malware signatures to detect suspicious software. This technology is reactive by nature and as a result lags behind the hacker's deployment speed and morphing abilities. What further complicates matters is that users don't always understand the need to keep their detection software updated. Given the volume of new malware entering the Internet each day, using either product with last week's signature files is akin to going into battle with a bow and arrow.

As security technicians, we're frequently amazed when an infected computer is uncovered and the first words out of the users' mouth are "I run (insert you're A/V product name here) at least once per month! How could this happen?" and we see that the signature file is 6 months out of date.

If your signature files are even an hour out-of-date, you're already hundreds of thousands of malware behind the development curve!

Compounding that problem is the fact that no single A/V or A/M product can detect everything. That's why any good security tech worth his salt uses a cocktail of multiple programs to scrub computers of malware and even then a full cleaning may require further manual investigative work to find all the culprits infecting your computer network.

Zero-Day Attacks -
Hackers Exploiting Software Vulnerabilities

What's a Zero Day Exploit?

That's a term that's used to describe malware or intrusion exploits that find a new vulnerability in specific piece of software regularly used in computers that's never been fixed or even known about by defenders before. It's called "a zero day" vulnerability because there's no reaction time to respond between the attack and the effort to fix the program.

Margaret Rouse, executive Director of "WhatIs" magazine defines zero day exploits this way. "A zero-day exploit is one that takes advantage of a security vulnerability on the same day that the vulnerability becomes generally known. There are zero days between the time the vulnerability is discovered and the first attack."

In spring of 2013, Oracle Software, one of the largest software companies in the world, got caught with their pants down when hackers detected a Zero Day defect in Java that took some time for Oracle to patch. Since almost every computer in the world uses Java, and since the vulnerability existing on almost every computer using Java in the world, exploiting that Zero-Day vulnerability caused massive havoc on the Internet. At the time, their alert to the industry said "These vulnerabilities may be remotely exploitable without authentication, i.e., they may be exploited over a network without the need for a username and password." The bug was first reported to Oracle early in February, 2013 but Oracle didn't plan to release the patch to fix it until March 13th and the hackers pounced during that lapse. OOPS!

Sometimes you'll get caught in situations like this but the more common instance is user PC's not being kept current on updates for the various software components used on them. That's why patching and updating computers is so important today. Microsoft regularly publishes updates to their operating systems twice each week and other companies like Adobe with Flash Player and Acrobat, Oracle with Java, Mozilla with Firefox, Google with Chrome and many, many others publish security updates on varying schedules. Update management is critical to protecting your network but it's still just one piece of the puzzle.

The Impact of BYOD, the Distributed Workforce and the CLOUD on your Network

The BYOD phenomenon has dramatically changed how business must consider network security. For those of you who have led a more sheltered existence and aren't yet familiar with BYOD, here's your new reality. Employees are bringing their portable computing devices to work and expect you to let them use them for their own and possibly business purposes. PDA, notebooks, tablets, smartphones are connecting to your network and you have to be conscious of what comes in with them and what may leave with them when those devices go back home.

Also, more employees are working from home or outside of the office. If you allow access to your network by these employees, clients or vendors, you have to consider how secure your portal that these people use is and how secure is <u>their</u> environment. The perimeter defense of your network can be wonderful but if you allow personal devices that are compromised to connect to your network, it's about the same as letting a Trojan Horse enter your network. What's in that computer you just let connect to your network? That also holds true for remote access workers. How secure is their computer? What can and will happen if you let them access your network, servers and other resources? There's a whole list of issues that you have to address when letting outsiders connect to your network whether they be consultants, customers, vendors or employees. Don't overlook this vulnerability in your next network audit.

Top Threats from Mobile Devices

1. Data Loss from lost, stolen, or decommissioned devices
2. Information stealing mobile malware
3. Data Loss and data leakage through poorly written third-party applications
4. Vulnerabilities within devices, OS, design, and third-party applications
5. Unsecured Wi-Fi, network access, and rogue access points
6. Unsecured or rogue marketplaces
7. Insufficient management tools, capabilities, and access to APIs
8. Near-field communications and proximity-based hacking

You also have to be aware of how your workforce might be using the cloud either with or without your permission. Want an example? Joe in your accounting department is very conscientious but not very tech savvy. He likes to take work home with him once in a while. He doesn't have a notebook or tablet but he does have a buddy with a free Amazon Cloud Space account and on occasion he uploads data from his work PC to the cloud to later retrieve it from home. His intentions are all noble but how secure is your data in that cloud? Who else has access to that cloud account? How malware free is his home PC and is it possible that when he brings that data back to the office there might be "a little something extra" riding along.

These are all potential malware entry points onto your network that aren't necessarily well addressed in traditional defense systems.

Remote access services (e.g., VNC, RDP) continue their rise in popularity, accounting for 88% of all breaches leveraging hacking techniques—more than any other external vector. How do you handle that access? What rules do you have in place when you allow it?

WHAT ABOUT FIREWALLS?
DON'T THEY STOP MALWARE?

Let's spend a couple of minutes talking about firewalls. There are 2 general types of firewalls – hardware firewalls and software firewalls. Software firewalls usually reside on the device you're trying to protect. The primary example is Windows Firewall which comes built into the Windows operating system of each PC.

The main problem with software firewalls is that they can't detect or fight a piece of malware until it's already in the network or on your computer. It's like defending your castle once the enemy has already entered the courtyard. The goal of a firewall should be to prevent an intruder of getting to the courtyard of your castle/network in the first place.

That's what hardware firewalls are intended to do. Your firewall should be positioned at the entry point to your network and should stop the intruder BEFORE it gets into your network. That's why the emperors of China built their great walls (or firewall) on the border of their territory and NOT just around their capital city. They wanted to keep the bad guys as far away from their cities as possible. Sure, the invaders got through occasionally, but the defenders had time to rally other counter measures to fight off the attack.

Building your defense system based upon a solely software firewall solution also requires a lot of constant attention and it still is a reactive way to defend against the "Mongolian Hordes" of Malware with no secondary line of defense from the throngs of hackers out there on the Internet hell-bent on looting your castle.

Are firewalls the answer to fighting a l intruders? Sorry, no. BUT they are a component you'll need to develop in a blended defense strategy to improve your defenses against malware, exploits and denial of service attacks.

Now, let's dig a little deeper into how firewalls are put together with respect to security. Normally, in their base configuration, most firewalls don't deal with malware specifically. Their base functions are traffic management and intrus on prevention based upon certain categories of traffic. While keeping my explanation as simple as possible, basic firewall functions can limit or restrict traffic to and from your network by IP address (Internet locations), or by port identifier (types of traffic) and set up secure communication between locations (tunneling and VPN etc.) That's about it. The cheaper the firewall, the more basic the functionality.

BUT . . . If, for example, you allow web traffic on your connection to the internet, without extra options added to your firewall, there's not much within that protocol that you can use to inspect and regulate that stream with a basic firewall. Most good firewalls do have extra features that can be added as options that can improve content management and inspection. Keep in mind that fighting malware is a constantly evolving process and what worked 5 years ago probably doesn't work very well now. If your firewall is over a few years old, chances are you're fighting a losing battle with outdated technology particularly if you haven't kept your firewall up-to-date with the latest firmware updates.

Some broadband providers offer embedded firewall services in their modems or routers. It's been my experience that these features are at best rudimentary and less thar ideal. Some providers also don't let you manage those devices so you become dependent upon them for settings, changes and updates. I strongly recommend you get your own firewa l device and have someone experienced in firewall management configure and maintain it for you. While the interfaces for firewalls may appear very easy to use, the concepts behind the interface are more complex than you might expect. It's not rocket science, but configuration is best left to someone with experience.

THE UTM FIREWALL – UNIFIED THREAT MANAGEMENT

In practice, UTM is the evolution of the traditional firewall into an all-inclusive security product able to perform multiple security functions within a single appliance: network firewalling, network intrusion prevention and gateway antivirus (AV), gateway anti-spam, VPN, content filtering, load balancing, data leak prevention and on-appliance reporting.

UTM advantages

1. Reduced complexity: Single security solution. Single Vendor. Single AMC
2. Simplicity: Avoidance of multiple software installation and maintenance
3. Easy Management: Plug & Play Architecture, Web-based GUI for easy management
4. Reduced technical training requirements, one product to learn.
5. Regulatory compliance

UTM Disadvantages

1. Single point of failure for network traffic
2. Single point of compromise if the UTM has vulnerabilities
3. Potential impact on latency and bandwidth when the UTM cannot keep up with the traffic

Built-in Threat Management takes the firewall process to the next level of protection rolling multiple components of Threat Detection into the firewall function. In a single device you can manage multiple threat detection engines but keep in mind that rarely will a UTM device provide best-of-breed features in each distinct function.

Think of these devices as the Swiss Army Knife of malware protection not a foolproof solution to every threat.

A word of caution before you buy a UTM firewall. Since a great percentage of your network traffic will be going through your UTM device be sure you get one with enough throughput capacity to handle your current traffic plus some room for growth. Firewall UTMs will process A LOT of data and if you purchase one with inadequate throughput, you run the risk of overwhelming the firewalls functional capacity and thereby slow performance on your network. Have a professional check your firewall throughput statistics before you buy a new device and make sure you buy one that is capable of handling your current throughput plus a good healthy margin more. Don't cheap out and buy the bottom of the product line. Most firewalls and UTM's are priced based upon their throughput capacity and built-in security features. Network throughput goes up every year so it's better to go high than cheap out and pick one that won't grow with your network just to save a few bucks now.

In order to have the highest levels of protection from advanced threats, your organization must be able to do these three essential things very effectively.

1.   Prevent even the most sophisticated attacks. Although many in the industry have redirected focus on detection, prevention remains crucial to effective enterprise security. Today's behavioral detection capabilities have come a long way from static signatures and are capable of identifying and then helping to prevent many previously unknown attacks, even those attempting to exploit Zero-Day vulnerabilities. In the same way we haven't abandoned a sound patch management strategy because of the number of vulnerabilities, we can't abandon the goal of prevention because of the sophistication or frequency of attacks.

2. Detect stealthy threats across the entire infrastructure. Beyond prevention, there is a clear need to be able to detect attacks that were not preventable and stop them from causing further harm. This means disrupting the attack chain and preventing any further compromises such as lateral movement, data exfiltration and the like. You can't rely solely in PC installed defense mechanisms like in the past.

3. Respond continuously to security incidents. Here's the key to effective defense. We must be able to quickly respond to the attack in the event that we were not effective at preventing it. We have to understand the incident and how to rectify and avoid similar issues in the future.

Rating Unified Threat Management Devices

For those of you who are new to the IT Security world, one of the top research organizations in the IT field is Gartner Research. Each year they analyze trends in our industry and produce reports about how providers are dealing with the challenges we face. As a summary graphic of their results they produce a chart called their "Magic Quadrant" in which they attempt to identify how vendors stack up in their respective fields. The chart identifies leaders and laggards based upon their ability to execute a complete solution in their category.

Using the Gartner Research rankings again, this time for UTM (Unified Threat Management) devices, let's see how the different vendors stacked up:

Ratings for Unified Threat Management Products	
Rankings	**Companies**
Industry Leaders	Fortinet Check Point Dell-SonicWall WatchGuard Sophos
Challengers	Cisco Juniper Networks
Visionaries	Cybercam Netasq
Niche Players	Huawei Gateprotect Clavister Keno
Source: Gartner Magic Quadrant for Unified Threat Management July 2013	

Keep in mind that you're looking at the chart for a Unified Threat Management devices blending multiple defense mechanisms in a single device. This doesn't mean, for example, that Fortinet has the top rated anti-virus solution when compared with a dedicated A/V product. It may, but then again, it may not stack up as the best against a single function A/V tool like Trend Micro or McAfee in that area. All-in-all, though, if you think of UTM as the Swiss Army Knife of Malware defense tools it does rate pretty well.

Your advantage with UTM is that you have only one tool to manage and maintain for multiple types of threats vs. finding and managing best-of-breed products across multiple threat levels.

Here's the key, though. Even UTM by itself isn't enough. Just like your network anti-virus program, it's only one piece of the puzzle. Using one product only is risky. If that device fails or malfunctions, you're defenseless. A blended approach with multiple defense mechanisms provides a more comprehensive defense methodology.

Our goal here is to keep the bad stuff as far away from your network and computers as possible not just remove them once they're on your network.

I have to inject a word of caution for these rankings. Each of these products does some component of Intrusion Prevention pretty well and these rankings are created by a blended score across all functions so a Fortinet doesn't necessarily do <u>everything</u> single process better than a Juniper but overall it was rated better based upon a blended score of ALL considerations. It also doesn't take into account base price and the cost of "options" that may be standard functions in other devices. For example, for years, Cisco has been notorious for making almost everything a paid option. For a while, even a parts and labor warranty for their devices was considered an "option". Fortinet, conversely, includes many features as standard that most of the others consider options for a fee.

Finally, I have to strongly caution against the impulse to use the "free" firewall features provided by broadband vendors. In many cases, the provider will not give you full access to it for fear you might make a mistake in configuration and then blame them so they'll withhold the gateway password. I also strongly advise against software firewalls and so-called "free" firewalls like Microsoft PC Firewall. The word free should be a dead giveaway. No product worth anything is FREE and you'll usually get less than your money's worth out of products in that category!

Advanced Threat Protection (ATP)

There are 100s of millions of malware variations, which makes it extremely challenging to protect organizations. While Advanced Intrusion activities are stealthy and hard to detect, the command and control network traffic associated with them can be detected at the network layer level. This requires comprehensive log analyses and log correlation from various sources. It's all about the logs. Agents can be used to collect logs (TCP and UDP) directly from assets into a syslog server. Then a Security Information and Event Management (SIEM) tool must analyze the data.

Gartner Research has identified 5 core styles of Advanced Threat Protection that can be used for network security protection against intrusion:

❖ **Style 1** – Use Network Traffic Analysis techniques to establish baselines of normal traffic patterns, (for example anomalous DNS traffic could indicate botnet traffic) and highlight anomalous patterns that represent a compromised environment. This approach offers real-time detection and can include both non-signature and signature-based techniques, and endpoint agents aren't required.

A sampling of vendors with products in this category would be Arbor Networks, Damballa, Fidelis, Lancope and Sourcefire's AMP, according to Gartner. (Sourcefire was recently acquired by Cisco).

❖ **Style 2** – Network Forensics typically provide "full-packet capture and storage of network traffic" as well as analytics and reporting tools for incident response of advanced threats. The advantages they bring include reducing incident response time and they can reconstruct and replay flows and events over days or weeks, along with sometimes offering detailed reports to meet regulatory requirements.

Among the vendors in Style 2 are said to be Blue Coat (Solera Networks) and RSA (NetWitness).

❖ **Style 3** – Payload Analysis can use a sandbox technique (either on premises or in the cloud) to detect targeted attacks on a near-real-time basis. but they typically don't the ability to track endpoint behavior over a period of days, weeks or months.

Examples of Style 3 would be AhlLab, Check Point with its Threat Emulation Software Blade, FireEye, Lastline, McAfee with its ValidEdge acquisition, Palo Alto Networks with Wildfire, ThreatGrid and Trend Micro with Deep Discovery, says Gartner.

❖ **Style 4** – Endpoint Behavior Analysis is based on the idea of "application containment to protect endpoints by isolating applications and files in virtual containers. Other innovations in this style include system configuration, memory and process monitoring to block attacks, and techniques to assist with real-time incident response." This Style 4 approach requires an agent on every endpoint, Gartner says. It can "intercept kernel system calls and block malicious activity such as thread injection attacks," and "by isolating Web browsing sessions, protect users from malicious websites, including drive-by download sites and 'watering holes.'"

The strength of this approach is blocking zero-day attacks, provides some basis forensics, and protecting systems whether they are on or off the network, but the challenge is that deploying and managing the agent software is operationally intensive and particularly hard in bring-your-own-device (BYOD) environments.

Examples of vendors here include Blue Ridge Networks, Bromium, Invincea, Sandoxie and Trustware. Vendors that support memory monitoring include Cyvera, ManTech/HBGary (Digital DNA) and RSA's Ecat.

❖ Style 5 – The last style in the Gartner style catalog is Endpoint Forensics, which involves tools for incident response teams. These endpoint agents collect data from hosts they monitor. They can help automate incident response and monitor hosts on and off corporate networks. The challenge in using them, though, is they can be operationally intensive to deploy and manage, and support for non-Windows endpoints is quite limited.

Examples of Style 5 vendors with tools include Bit9, Carbon Black, Guidance Software EnCase Analytics, Mandiant and ManTech/HBGary's Responder Pro.

Your problem with ATM as a small to medium sized organization is the support effort and associated costs of a full-fledged ATM solutions using these stand-alone products. Most small business can't afford the dedicated IT Security staff to monitor and manage a complex environment like this. Some of these products prices have been pegged at "north of $100k"

An appropriate alternative might be to out-source your security processes to a skilled security services organization that can protect your network from a centralized security monitoring center using their software on a software-as-a-service (SAAS) pricing model. In this manner, you can get the best of both worlds – a lower cost of ownership while gaining the advantage of a well-trained security team keeping watch. Your only real dilemma then becomes identifying the skilled practitioners from the "wanna-be's". Here's where references and training certifications become your all-important benchmark. This is no place for the self-taught or the "friend of a friend"!

One of the recurring industry jokes that is sadly based upon reality was that the company IT expert was unavailable because the local elementary school classes didn't end until 3:30 pm. In my experience, many non-profits rely on volunteers hoping to save money. In some instances, the volunteers qualifications may be little more than being able to spell IT.

As in many occupations, practitioners of IT can have many specialties and being qualified in one does certainly doesn't guarantee competency in another. Whether it's an outside consultant or an applicant for an in-house technical position, it's important to check references for all technical positions. There are too many "so-called" IT security specialists who can "talk the talk" but can't "walk the walk" as the expression goes. There is absolutely nothing wrong with asking a candidate to "prove it!".

Don't Dismiss the Effectiveness of Social Engineering

Social Engineering comes in many guises. The most common attempts come in as e-mail requests for recipients to confirm information for an organization they may recognize. The hacker will attempt to trick the user into believing that a link in the e-mail will connect them to a secure banking or financial site to confirm receipt of some data. Instead it will route them to a carefully crafted "alternative" sight used to harvest personal or company information.

Other times, hackers may attempt to trick an employee over the phone into revealing some personal or company information like a password, a co-worker name or some type of contact information that the hacker can then use with other data gathered to exploit your network.

Malware may be used to create pop-ups that look like legitimate network warning messages that might prompt for a password or other security information that will then be transferred to a command and control computer off-premises for further use later.

Some of those most common social engineering tricks that hackers use in e-mail are:

1. Deposit confirmations from xyz bank
2. Order confirmations
3. Shipping or delivery confirmations from FedEx, UPS etc.
4. Requests for security confirmation from xyz financial institution
5. Shared pictures from a friend
6. E-mail from "tech support"

Let's not forget the unsolicited fake phone calls from "tech support" or "the HR department". You need to constantly remind your staff who should and shouldn't be recognized on the phone. Tell them that when they're in doubt, they should ask for a call-back phone number and use it to confirm the caller's identity. Few Social Engineers will ever provide their phone number.

Recently, we've seen an increased frequency of supposed tech support reps saying they're calling from Microsoft support or Yahoo or Google support. Trust me, those support companies DON'T call users unsolicited. Heck, most times they don't even return phone calls let alone initiate them!

Recently I was helping a client who reported that their accounting computer was running very slowly, a not uncommon symptom of spyware or malware infection. As I was removing the spyware, the client's phone rang and she answered it. After a moment, with a confused look on her face, she handed the phone to me saying that it was "Microsoft Tech Support" calling to report that they had noticed "suspicious Internet traffic" coming from her computer and they wanted to help remove malware. Let me stop right here and say that Microsoft DOES NOT ever call users to offer tech support unsolicited! But, I was intrigued so I took the phone and played along as the user of the PC. The caller was very smooth and very reasonable explaining that he was "just trying to help" and would I mind if we set up a remote access session so he could clean my computer. I played along for a while but never let him have access. In the end, the caller was looking to install malware on the user's PC to collect data or for some other illegal purpose.

I have to admit that this hacker worked from a well-practiced script and I can understand where some inexperienced computer users could fall prey to this technique. I strung him along for a while just to play with him and see what I could learn but in the end, I terminated the call and reinforced with my client that they should never respond to any so-called tech support offers from anyone or any organization that they don't have a personal relationship with.

After that, I received reports from other clients of people posing as representatives from Microsoft, Google and Yahoo tech support offering unsolicited help. Hackers are becoming bolder and bolder and to borrow a phrase once used by AT&T, they "Reach out and touching someone" in person instead of just hiding in the shadows of the Internet.

Building Your Multi-Layered Network Defense System

OK, let's get down to building your multi-layer defense strategy. I've spent a good deal of time building a history of malware and the inherent problems with traditional malware detection systems, now it's time to lay out how to fix your system and build a better defense mechanism for the future of your network.

Here's how you should approach building up your defenses:

Step 1 – Addressing e-mail borne malware

Add additional e-mail scrubbing levels to your e-mail

Sniff out Malware BEFORE it reaches your network!

Since about 50% of malware intrusion attempts start with infected e-mail, make every attempt to get those scrubbed before they even enter your environment. Invest in a good, off-premises (aka cloud) A/V, A/M, anti-phishing and anti-spam solution. Most of the top-tier A/V providers offer an advanced version of their software that includes off-site e-mail scrubbing so for a few dollars more on your annual A/V subscription you can easily add an off-premises spam/malware scrubbing system.

Keeping malware out of your system as your first step will greatly reduce your exposure to malware and phishing e-mail traffic. PLUS it has the added bonus of reducing traffic on your Internet connection. How? Most experts agree that about 95% of all e-mail is spam and the traffic generated by all of this junk can create a burden on your Internet connection. If you can stop most of this junk BEFORE it even hits your router by sniffing out malware and removing it in the cloud that's all for the better. Don't think for a second, though, that this will totally solve your e-mail malware problem. This is only the first step and you must create as many obstacles as possible to deter Hackers intent on penetrating your network.

Step 2 – Strengthening your perimeter defenses

Build a Better Perimeter Firewall and add UTM

Remember, firewall technology is evolved a great deal in recent

years to include additional detection techniques. Replacing a simple firewall with a good UTM firewall can make all the difference between infection and resistance. Resist the urge that many fall into. It's that false sense of security that now that you've put something in place, you can now relax. This sucker has to be maintained and monitored frequently. Your network motto should always be "semper vigilans" – ALWAYS vigilant. UTM devices must be constantly monitored and updated. Letting your guard down by not paying attention to your UTM could spell disaster if the wrong malware leaks through because you didn't pay attention and keep it up-to-date!

This is not the place to cheap out! This is your business we're trying to protect. How much is your business worth? If one ransomware software gets through your defenses, your potential loss could cost you everything and never believe that "It will never happen here!" It does and it will. Remember, it's not a matter of IF you'll be hit but just a matter of WHEN!

Make sure you add an additional layer of protection with anti-virus installed here as well. Don't fool yourself into thinking that "Oh, I've got A/V installed on my PC's. That should be enough!" When fighting Malware, there's no such thing as enough. Most UTM/Firewall vendors will offer a different A/V solution than your desktop A/V vendor so adding this additional resource to your tools to fight malware thus closing the exposure window just a little bit more.

Step 3 – Watch for atypical traffic that might reveal infections

Network Traffic and Behavior Monitoring

Analyze Network traffic for signs of Malware

Let's keep working out way into your network. Next you should be looking at some of the features within any good UTM device to track unusual activity from your computing devices.

While malware signatures change to avoid detection, the core characteristics of how they behave once they're on your network remain pretty consistent. Trojans that communicated with command and control servers still act the same way and you can watch for that activity not just its "signature". The same is true of other types of malware that send spam and such. Even if you fail to catch them as they enter your network, you still have a chance to track them down and remove them if you know how your network performs normally so that any up-tick in various types of communication traffic can indicate abnormal activity that might indicate a previously undetected infection.

Best security practices dictate that you establish a baseline for network and Internet traffic on your network using the tools in your firewall/UTM or some other traffic analysis mechanism and watch your traffic analyzer to detect when out of the ordinary traffic flows might indicate that one of your devices is "going rogue" and communicating with an off-premises command and control computer. While signatures of malware change frequently, how they act and communicate don't. This could be your big tip that your network is infected.

Step 4 – Manage BYOD Devices that might infect your network

Employee Device Management

Managing employee devices on your network

In my experience, the smaller the organization, the more likely they are to neglect the issue of BYOD – employee devices on the network. By allowing employees to bring their devices to work without any sort of controls in place greatly increases your risk that something will go wrong. An employee that brings his or her notebook to work, with all of the good intentions in the world to "do a little extra work at home", could be bringing an infected PC right past your malware protection system.

Let me be blunt. With rare exceptions your staff are not IT security experts. Can you really rely on their personally chosen A/V solution to meet the standards needed for your network?

If you let your employees use your email system on their smartphones and tablets, you risk infection "by proxy" if you don't require some sort of security be installed on their devices regardless of device type. Portables and

Smartphones are becoming a very high-profile hacker target precisely because individuals are so lax in securing those devices.

If you explain your reasons clearly in an "Employee Personal Device Use" policy and establish a program for securing those devices properly, you shouldn't have a big problem implementing some common sense security measures.

Your bottom line should be "If you're going to access my resources, your device has to be secure and you have to follow a few simple rules about security."

Step 5 - Establish access protocols for Remote Access

Remote Access Security Practices

Remote Computing Management

As we said earlier, staff members that work in a non-traditional workplace off-premises is an ever growing segment of today's workforce. Taking advantage of the flexibility that gives your business requires some steps to secure that access method.

At the very least, your remote workers should be using a secure access method that requires two levels of password authentication and a sophisticated level of data encryption to protect that communication. There are vendors like Citrix, VMware and even Microsoft that can deliver that level of security. If you're looking for something a little more affordable, you can use some of the built-in VPN (virtual private network) functionality in most good firewalls to create a secure link between locations.

If your remote users are in a static location like a branch office, you can create a secure point-to-point virtual private network (VPN) between the firewalls in each location with high level encryption. Your firewalls handle the security and encryption and then the workstations off-site can use the network login and password security of your network to authenticate your users.

If your employee is mobile and requires connecting to your network from anywhere at any time, you can use a VPN client installed on their PC to first authenticate against the VPN rules of the firewall, again with encryption rules you define, and then a second login to your network. This creates a dual layer of identity authentication plus a high level of encryption that's under your control.

Using Remote Desktop technology, your employees actually use a desktop platform defined on your server and don't use their PC's as anything more than a dumb terminal when accessing your network. This improves performance by reducing data traffic back and forth across the connection plus reduces your exposure to any infections that may exist on your employee's computer.

I strongly advise against trying to use PC's to connect to your network as a workstation on the network. Not only does it increase your risk of cross infection from that off-premises computer, it may turn out that your programs will run very badly due to bandwidth limitations as a result.

Step 6 – Flash Drives and Portable Device Management

Portable Devices

Portable storage devices like flash drives pose a two-fold threat to business networks. First, they can be an easy to hide conveyance vehicle to remove sensitive data from your building undetected. The second risk is the potential of employees bringing an infection into your network from home.

The risk of data leaving your network undetected

There are two basic ways to handle controlling how information leaves your network and you can use either one. It's up to you. Security software from companies like Checkpoint can encrypt all data written to removable media whether it's flash drives, CDs or DVDs. In this manner, you can provide authorized users with a changeable encryption key to data they need to take off-site and if they misplace the device your data is still unreadable to those unauthorized people that don't have the key. There is a cost to that solution but its nominal compared to the risk of doing nothing.

The other alternative is to simply shut down the use of USB drives and writing to your CD drives by setting prohibitive rules at either the Group Policy level of your network or at the PC level. This may seem a bit Draconian but there's virtually no cost involved. Trust me on this, using Group Policy is much easier to manage.

Step 7 – Control the risk of malware entry via portable devices

To demonstrate your potential exposure, here's a real example of an organization that suffered catastrophic data loss precisely because of a lax attitude towards the use of flash drives on their network.

A local private school encouraged their staff members to take data back and forth from the office to work from home. One employee unwittingly brought in a flash drive infected with a malware that attempted to erase all data it came in contact with.

To make matters worse, the malware used an auto-run trigger to start-up the malware as soon as the location where it resided was addressed by any local computer user anywhere on the network. The malware spread like wildfire onto every drive and folder it could "see" on the network. When the employee accessed the data on the flash drive from the schoo PC, it installed itself on the local C: drive and erased all of the data there. It then installed itself on all of the mapped network drives that the employee had permission to access and began erasing data there too. When another employee on the network accessed the same network drive, it instead found the auto-run trigger loaded there and it immediately began erasing that users' local hard drive and any additional network mapped drives that the second employee had access to that the first employee did not. In a matter of 45 minutes or so, almost all of the data on the school network was virtually gone as well as any local data stored on any workstation that connected to the network server.

The school business manager called our office in a panic exclaiming "I'm watching all of our data disappearing before my very eyes!" and she was right.

We rushed on-site and found the source of the problem but the damage was already done. The server was wiped out and approximately 120 workstations were infected. No, their anti-virus program didn't catch the malware. It took most A/V companies 4-5 days to react to this particular outbreak and publish a solution but that was 4 days too late for this school.

Of course, we disinfected all of the impacted computers manually, restored all of their lost data because, thankfully, they had used our recommended backup solution.

We then collected EVERY flash drive in the organization and scrubbed them too.

The final irony to the conclusion of my story? The employee that brought the infection into the network on his flash drive swore that we were wrong and it wasn't his fault but after getting the cleaned flash drive back from us, he brought in another infected flash drive and the same thing happened again 3 days later (before the A/V vendors published their solution). Finally, after the second infection, the school administrators relented and let us put some security rules in place to stop further intrusions like this.

Turning off all USB functionality is a rather draconian step but it's the cleanest and cheapest remedy to the problem. Unfortunately, it can be a productivity killer and unless you turn off everyone's CD drives as well you still have an exposure to risk.

To handle this type of issue, there are several steps you can take if you're not willing to just disable the USB ports on all of your computers. First, make sure your IT staff turns off all auto-run functionality on all CD and DVD drives as well as USB drives. Auto-run is the operating system feature that will automatically detect and execute certain file types on portable devices. You've seen it work when you put a CD into a drive and it automatically starts up the program on the CD It is intended to automatically run whatever program resides on that device. Turning off auto-run is a relatively easy task. Then set your anti-virus product to immediately inspect any new media connected to the computer BEFORE allowing access to that media.

Step 8 – Control and Monitor Your Wireless Network

Protecting Wireless Access

Secure Wireless Networks

There are several ways that wireless hackers/malware can explcit your network and one of the most common ways is technical misconfiguration of your wireless that allows unauthorized access by non-employees and outsiders.

Let's start with the basics

The first mistake some people make is thinking that just because you don't give someone a login ID and password to your server that they can't get into your network via wireless. That's wrong! It may slow up the process a little but not by much.

First and foremost in wireless is the need to separate users of your wireless into Private and Public access users. Some of your users only need access to your Internet access and/or your printers, for example – visiting guests Some others may need access to your programs or the data on your server, for example – your employees. These would be Private users. Segmenting your wireless network into separate virtual Private and Public networks (VLANs) that can't even see one another keeps these two kinds of users apart. In this way your visitors can access the Internet for their purposes while your employees can access their portion of the wireless network which can "see" and access the resources they need.

Wireless networks are identified by portable devices by a signal broadcast that is called an SSID. The SSID (Service Set Identifier) differentiates one WLAN (wireless local access network) from another, so all access points and all devices attempting to connect to a specific WLAN must use the same SSID to enable effective communication.

SSIDs should not be broadcast and should be suppressed to hide your network from view. Remember, unlike your wired network, your wireless network is not limited by the walls of your business. Broadcasting your SSID's is an open invitation to intruders to begin trying to hack your environment. This isn't necessarily an anti-malware tactic. It's more a basic anti-intrusion/hacking protection practice.

Even your Public wireless access network need not broadcast the SSID, again because it's an open invitation to hackers to try to exploit your network. If you want to give guests access to your network, it's a much better move to have small cards printed that provide the current Public SSID and authorization code. Don't turn off your wireless access rule that requires authorization codes just to make it easy for your guests. It only makes it easier for hackers to use your Internet connection for improper activities that may later be tracked back to you.

Did you ever notice in the movies that whenever a villain needs to use the Internet for nefarious purposes they use a cyber-café with free Internet access? Don't make your business parking lot a free cyber-café by broadcasting an open SSID without a password!

Once you've set up a hidden/un-broadcast Public access SSID with a password, don't get lazy and never change that password. Best Security Practices dictate that you regularly change your wireless passwords. Failing to do that opens your Wi-Fi up to the acts of vengeful ex-employees or disgruntled business associates who know that last month's password will still work.

On the Private side of your wireless access, after you require a password to access your wireless network, remember to require a valid personalized network password to access network resources. Please refer to the Section "Network and Server Maintenance" for more detailed suggestions on network security rules. Again, don't get lazy and use just one network login ID and password for everyone.   Of all of the failings that I've seen on client networks over the years, this is near the top of my list as the most frustratingly dumb things that I see in client environments. What is the point of a security system if everyone uses the same Login ID and password?

Step 9 – Backup, Backup, Backup!!! Then Test, Test, Test !!!

Data Protection and Backup

By far the most important component of network protection from hacking and malware is keeping a secure copy of all of your business critical data. This is also one of the most neglected areas in my experience in the field. This is NOT the place to cheap out but I am consistently stunned when I hear smart business people say "Oh, I don't want to spend over $xx.xx on backing up my server." A hacker exploiting a poor connection to erase your data, an employee taking revenge on you or a tornado throwing your server all the way to Kansas will create chaos and a good copy of all your data kept in a secure location that can be retrieved easily will save your business every time. Failing to do that one basic step can be the difference between recovery and the failure of your business. According to a study by Price Waterhouse Cooper, statistics show that about 70% of all businesses that experience a data disaster never recover and close their doors within 2 years.

How much you backup is really a function of what data you can live without and for how long. What do I mean by that? Here's are two simple examples of the differing needs for getting lost data back very quickly. What if a senior living center lost the contents of the server that contains the medications lists for all of their residents to a malware that erased their data. How long could they function without that information before their residents would be in jeopardy? Hours? Minutes? Certainly they could not wait days to get their data back!

On the other hand, an insurance office might be able to struggle along for a day or two without their data files in a pinch before their business was at risk.

Either way, both organizations would be in trouble without their data. It's just a matter of timing.

As I pointed out previously, it's not a matter of if you'll fall victim to malware intrusion or hacking it's just a matter of when. Don't get the false sense of security if you do everything in this book and more that you'll be totally safe from malware. There is always a risk that one will sneak through the most well maintained defenses. You have to be prepared just in case the worst happens so that you can still recover. That means backing up your data and keeping it safe.

What good would a section on data protection be without a good horror story, right?

A new client called me recently asking for help removing a Ransomware infection from their server. For those of you who haven't heard about this type of malware, it encrypts the contents of most of your hard drive with sophisticated high-level encryption and demands a ransom to provide the key to un-do the damage it did. Another IT company had thrown up their hands and walked away from the server after many hours and no solution. Removing the ransomware wasn't that hard but when we asked for their backup copy to restore the 99,000 encrypted data files, the client handed us a tape that didn't have any data on it. OOPS! We checked their other tapes. Again, Nothing! We checked their backup logs and their backup hadn't worked in years. There wasn't any valid backup data to restore. They never checked to make sure the backup worked! They "trusted the system". Double OOPS! For the first time in the history of our company, we had to put a malware BACK onto a computer after it had been removed because the client's only alternative was to pay the ransom and hope that the hacker would provide the key to unscrambling their data. After jumping through myriad technical hoops to pay the ransom, the key was provided but the decryption process ran for 5 days during which the staff sat around waiting because all of their work product was trashed. In the end, the client got about 95% of their data back after 6 days of lost company productivity but still lost 5% of their most critical business data. The moral of our story? Backing isn't enough unless you test to make sure it worked and you can recover your data if something goes wrong.

Step 10 – Patches, Updates and Software Management

Network and Server Maintenance

I recently read an interesting article about a correlation between Windows XP and the levels of spam on the Internet. The essence was that users that are still running Windows XP months after all Microsoft support has been cut off demonstrate how lax people are on keeping their security patches and updates up to date. Even at this late date, industry experts report that 25% of installed computers worldwide are still running Windows XP. If they can't even keep their operating system up-to-date, what are the odds that they pay attention to patch management?

Unpatched and unsupported computer software leads to higher levels of malware infection which supports hacker activity and ultimately causes an increase in spam volume on the Internet.

Let's talk about passwords

I recently conducted a security training for a local client staff meeting and when I got around to talking about using secure passwords, I took an informal poll of how many in attendance used the 10 most commonly guessed passwords on the Internet. I asked attendees to raise their hands if they used the password as I read them off. Before I got through the first 5 on the list over half of the audience had their hands up.

Passwords are the most basic step in business network security yet I am amazed at the number of times that business managers don't enforce even this most basic security step.

All computer networks should have centrally managed password rules with some level of complexity and renewal provisions.

Here are some basic rules for user passwords:

1. Require a minimum of 6 characters in passwords
2. Require at least one number and one special character in passwords
3. Make your users change their passwords at least quarterly
4. Make sure that users can't use the same password repeatedly

Don't allow users to share passwords and make sure no one ever post their passwords in view and nobody other than the network administrator should have the administrator's password.

You can't imagine how many times we encounter password on Post-It note attached to monitors or taped to the bottom of keyboards!

Step 11 – Centralize control of security rules and management

Using Group Policy Rules on your network

The best way to enforce security rules on your network is via Windows Group Policy or an equivalent central control system. This allows centralized control of password rules, network resources mapping and software updating. Trying to control or manage security at the PC level is inconsistent, unreliable and time-consuming but it's surprising sometimes how many network managers fall back on this inefficient practice.

Control what programs get loaded on your local computers and on the server

The best way to keep your software under control is to use centralized rules to remove unwanted software, update software and keep security tight. Some "old school" network administrators prefer to update software by going from PC to PC instead of centralizing their control for a variety of reasons. Unfortunately, in some instances that may be because they don't know how use the controls in the newer versions of the network operating system, sometimes they're just trying to stay busy but sometimes it's because the systems they are supporting are so out of date that they are forced to do it that way. All of these reasons have to be addressed if you're to run an efficient and properly protected security system.

Keep your apps and patches up-to-date across the network

Keeping your computers secure requires making sure that all software components on each PC are current and up-to-date. We're not just talking about just Microsoft Windows updates. Many malware exploits take advantage of out of date software that supports your Internet browsing activities regardless of which browser you use. Don't think that just because you use Firefox or Google Chrome instead of Internet Explorer that you're safe from Malware. Hackers target Oracle products like Java, Adobe products like Acrobat, Flash Player and other utilities used by all browsers. Yes, even Apple Safari!

It is critical that each device on your network be kept up-to-date including employee computers and smartphones. More and more hackers are turning their attention to portable devices precisely because they are security nightmares for organizations. Few users pay much attention to securing their portables and are prime hunting grounds for hackers.

Step 12 – Review data retention rules and access policies at least annually

Data Governance

Frequently, network servers can become an "elephant's graveyard" of sorts for old, out-of-date information that just never gets deleted. To some management types, it's just easier to buy more hard drives than it is to sit down and development a data management plan to sort through what can and cannot be eliminated.

What does it matter if you hold onto everything forever? Regulations require some data to be held for specific periods of time whether it's Sarbanes-Oxley, the IRS or HIPAA but total disregard for prudent data retention rules will only increase your risk of exposure because the more records you expose regardless of age, the greater your penalty could be. Trust me, penalties are being assessed and some are whoppers!

Also, the more data you retain, the hard it becomes to keep track of what's important and where it is kept. If your network is breached and your data storage is out of control, it will be that much harder to ascertain your exposure. If you're the target of a lawsuit and you can't segregate relevant for non-relevant data your exposure to discovery research goes up exponentially!

Here's another chilling thought brought to you by the always popular legal profession. Legal Discovery! If you're ever involved in litigation and you can't separate our "relevant" information when presented with a subpoena, the other party may have access to ALL of your data even the data that isn't critical to the issue. The same can also happen in an audit and other circumstances where you don't keep a proper handle on your data.

Step 13 – Whenever possible encrypt sensitive data

Data Encryption and your "data at rest"

Sensitive or confidential information protected by regulation should also be stored in encrypted format. In the early days, data stored in an SQL data base might have been considered sufficiently protected but not anymore. A relatively new term is being used by regulatory agencies to describe data storage methods. Now, "data at rest" (meaning stored on <u>ANY</u> media) is expected to be encrypted, even on your server! There are many tools available to do that and some are quite expensive. Fortunately, Microsoft Windows Server comes with a nice encryption tool called BitLocker and it doesn't cost a dime extra. If your confidential data is stored in a BitLocker encrypted storage area, your data is safer than it otherwise would be.

Step 14 - Staff Training and the use of Consultants

This step can't be stressed enough because a great part of hacking and malware is focused on "social engineering". Those are the attempts to fool computer users into doing something that they shouldn't do. Whether it's an e-mail with an embedded Trojan that will infect their PC or it's a phone call from a fake tech support representative, it's important to keep training your employees on what to watch for and what is and isn't expected of them as members of your organization.

Try to get in the habit of including a session on security issues in each staff meeting. Include Internet Safety Tips in every newsletter not only for your staff but also for business partners that may use or interface with your network.

If you delegate responsibility for a security process, Train First!

Over the years, I've noticed one consistent pattern in organizations when it comes to backing up systems and monitoring results. Inevitably, the job will be delegated to the lowest member on the corporate totem pole and the function becomes a practice of mindless rote with little understanding of what to look for or how the process even works. I can't express the number of times that we've walked into a network disaster and when we ask the question "Have you been checking on the backup (or A/V results reporting)?", we're greeted with a blank stare and we find out that so-and-so has changed the backup tape every morning for years but never once checked to see if it actually did anything.

In one instance, a victim of the ransomware CryptoLocker had studiously changed the company backup tape every day for 5 years but when the actually needed to use it we discovered that their tape drive had stopped writing for the entire time. There has to be formal training when responsibility for such an important task transfers from one employee to another and there has to be follow through. In this organizations case, they had no backup and no choice but to pay the hacker ransom and wait 5 days for the malware to recover the 100,000 destroyed files.

Don't rely on hands-on experience as your only training tool for your in-house staff. Very often, we see organizations authorize installing new security technology and then expect their in-house staff to figure out how it works and how to maintain it on their own or worse yet, bring a friend of a friend whose only real qualification may be that they knew how to spell Malware but not much more. Network management and security is a specialized skill set and not everyone is qualified to work in that area. Invest in training your staff to use your new technology properly. Newer security technology can be conceptually more complex and just because it has a nice, new spiffy interface doesn't mean that everything will magically get configured properly. Put some funds into your budget for training both for the initial installation and for on-going maintenance and support.

Training to battle the Social Engineering Threat

The key to combating social engineering is education. You need to frequently reinforce with your staff the importance of never falling prey to ALL types of social engineering whether by e-mail, by phone or in-person.

Constantly reinforce with them that if they're unsure of the veracity of the caller, ask for a call-back number and a referral contact and check them out before they return the call.

Using In-house staff vs. Outside consultants

Performing security audits

Not too long ago, we were invited to perform a network security audit for an organization. Their tech support team was confident that they had protected their environment thoroughly. In truth the in-house staff had put some nice security features in place but overall the security and protection of the network was pretty weak. At the review meeting to present the results of our audit, they were shocked at how easily we penetrated their network and the holes in security we found. In-house staff can have a built-in bias to believe that their efforts are the best and are really qualified to "break" what they built. Any outsider won't have that limitation.

A common flaw in testing of any kind when the in-house staff (or creators) are involved is that they have a tendency to test with the intent to prove their process works NOT to try to break their creation and demonstrate what doesn't work. That's why it's always better to have an outsider evaluate your security or at least someone outside of "the team".

Regulatory compliance may dictate that your organization must conduct security audits. I strongly advise against attempting to satisfy this need with in-house personnel. With rare exception, your staff is too close to the situation and won't be able to properly evaluate the vulnerabilities of what they built and maintain. You really need a fresh set of eyes that have more experience in environments other than your own. The goal of a security audit is to stress test the limitations of your security process and break it open if possible. In that way, you know where your vulnerabilities are located.

In-house staff vs. hiring outside Security Specialists

Hiring outsiders for technical support can be a great cost saver in the long run even though their hourly fee will appear to be much higher than your in-house staffing pay scale. The advantage financially is that you only have to pay your consultant for the hours actually worked on a given task. To put it bluntly – Is it better to employ an already trained security engineer to work a couple of hours per week to review your security conditions or have someone in-house that is poorly trained doing a half-assed job for a full-time paycheck? If you're not going to spend the money for skills training for your staff, it's better to hire an outsider to do the job correctly.

A number of years ago, one of my clients wanted to hire one of my technicians. The tech saw it as a great opportunity and the client was certainly willing to pay him a lot of money to move. A few months later, I got a call from the client asking for help on a complex issue so I visited the client's office and found my former tech shoveling snow outside the office. The problem was more complex than the current skillset for my guy so they still had to call in someone else to deal with that issue. As it turned out, the client didn't have enough work to keep their new tech busy so he spent a good percentage of his day working in the warehouse with others that made about 1/3 of what he was paid just to fill his day. Just because you have 20 computers doesn't mean your need to hire an expensive network technician who is heavily experienced in intrusion protection and network security. Sometimes is much more affordable to have an expert that some else has to pay the training expenses for to perform periodic security tasks for you.

Let's not forget the Cloud

There continues to be a lot of buzz about the cloud. Should you go there or shouldn't you?

Of course, the primary consideration of going to the cloud is the functionality of the process you're thinking about performing there but security and malware vulnerability should always remain major concern. Don't ever just assume that the cloud is always more secure than your local environment! Of course, the sales rep is going to claim great security but is it really? Your problem as a business manager is know the technical questions to ask to insure that your data is protected from all possible vulnerabilities.

Perhaps the most visible process that has been "in the cloud" for years is e-mail services. Whether or not you're considering Microsoft Office 365 e-mail, G-mail, Yahoo or any of the hundreds of others, public access email is a vulnerability you must face. How often have they had data stolen or accounts compromised? Before you entrust one of your most potentially vulnerable communications processes you should seriously dig into which cloud email provider to entrust your e-mail. You'd be amazed at the dismal security track records of some of the biggest names in the cloud industry.

Let's not forget that you should also exercise some control over employee access to public access e-mail providers. There's not much point in buttoning down your corporate e-mail system if you're going to allow your staff unfettered access to e-mail from a vendor of questionable filtering ability. An infected e-mail from an employee Hotmail account can be just as destructive to your network without proper precautions.

Just because the interface is web-enabled doesn't make the infection any less severe. You should consider using content filtering at your firewall level to block access to Internet e-mail portals, if not altogether then at least block some of the more blatantly insecure.

Here's an additional consideration. Most if not all of the so-called "free" email services like G-mail scan incoming and outgoing e-mail for meaningful content that can be re-distributed for profit. Google, the owner of Gmail, has gone as far as stating publicly that users of public email services should have no expectations of privacy. Data mining of content held on Google servers is a big profit center for that company and if you intend to communicate private information via g-mail or any other similar service you must keep that in mind. While you may object to the idea of data mining particularly with your information, Google cites an existing Supreme Court decision that permits data mining without permission in Smith v. Maryland, a 1979 Supreme Court decision that upheld the collection of electronic communications without a warrant.

Does that give you reason to pause before using Google Apps, for example, as a repository of business data in the future? It should! If you're going to put your processes or data in the cloud, you need written assurances from any provider before contracting with them to store your information.

Additional questions about security policies, data encryption, backup and recovery procedures also need to be dealt with. If you're not sufficiently well versed in what questions need to be asked and answered, I strongly recommend that you contract with a security consultant to perform those tasks for you.

I predict you'll find a wide disparity between what vendors promise and what they actually deliver. Over the years, I've seen outwardly rock solid cloud-based processes blow up in the faces of customer due to improperly researched applications with large and small cloud providers.

Summary

If there's one thing that I want you to take away from reading this book, it's that Malware Protection and Network Security are not a "fix it and forget it" proposition. It's a constantly changing landscape and will require constant attention and a series of adjustment as the battle against intruders goes on over time.

Remember also that Malware protection is not a single barrier that you can throw up and forget about. If you fall into the trap of that mindset, it's only a matter of time before your business falls prey to hackers and data thieves.

You have to think of malware protection as a layered defense mechanism where it's important to create as many different obstacles for intruders that are intent of breaking down your defenses. No single vendor has the magic bullet that can eliminate all threats no matter what the sales rep tells you. As I stated at the very beginning of this book, your network motto should always be "semper vigilans" – ALWAYS vigilant. The minute you let your guard down could be the moment the bad guys break through.

I've identified 14 steps that you can take to better protect your network. It's not a matter of picking your favorite and moving forward with that single step or even a couple of steps. It should be a matter of implementing as many of these as possible. The more roadblocks you can put between those that are determined to penetrate your network and your most valuable resources, your data, the better off you'll be as an organization.

Keep in mind that security is a constantly changing world and it's important to keep ahead of whatever those intruders will try next. What worked last year or even last month might not work tomorrow. If you don't have the time or patience to keep up on the attack vector changes that are inevitably going to happen, be prepared to hire someone who can do that for you.

Remember the figures I used earlier. There were more malwares and viruses published in 2013 that in the previous 25 years and that exponential growth will only increase.

Whenever a new countermeasure is introduced by the A/V defense forces to defeat the current intrusion threats, you can count on the Intruders at the Gates to counter that with even more creative attacks. This battle is only to get tougher in the future. Get Ready and Good Luck!

Glossary

Administrator Back Doors

This kind of attack is akin to stealing the building master keys from the building janitor: the perpetrator accesses the system as if they were an entrusted employee. In the case of computer administrators: special all-access accounts allow the user into areas where only trusted network administrator should go. These administrator areas include password recovery options. If the hacker can enter your system with the administrator's account, the hacker can retrieve passwords of most anyone on that system.

Advanced Persistent Threat (APT)

APT is a set of stealthy and continuous computer hacking processes, often orchestrated by human(s) targeting a specific entity. APT usually targets organizations and or nations for business or political motives. APT processes require high degree of covertness over a long period of time. As the name implies, APT consists of three major components/processes: advanced, persistent, and threat. The advanced process signifies sophisticated techniques using malware to exploit vulnerabilities in systems. The persistent process suggests that an external command and control is continuously monitoring and extracting data off a specific target. The threat process indicates human involvement in orchestrating the attack.

Advanced Volatile Threats (AVT)

Advanced Volatile Threats (AVT) are an advanced kind of cyber-attack where the malicious code does not need to reach its victim's hard drive in order to deliver its payload. Typically, AVTs exploit RAM resident programs and apps like Java and similar applications which also make them threats to most major operating systems including Apple OSx.

Traditional antivirus solutions depend on the presence of a file on the hard drive. That particularity makes this attack more potent and more difficult to detect and remove.

Botnet

A botnet is a collection of Internet-connected programs communicating with other similar programs in order to perform tasks. This can be as mundane as keeping control of an Internet Relay Chat (IRC) channel, or it could be used to send spam email or participate in distributed denial-of-service attacks. The word botnet is a combination of the words robot and network. The term is usually used with a negative or malicious connotation.

Brute Force Attack

Brute force is about overpowering the computer's defenses by using repetition. In the case of password hacking, dictionary attacks involve dictionary software that recombines English dictionary words with thousands of varying combination. (Yes, much like a Hollywood safecracker movie scene, but much slower and much less glamorous). Brute force dictionaries always +start with simple letters "a", "aa", "aaa", and then eventually moves to full words like "dog", "doggie", "doggy". These brute force dictionaries can make up to 50 attempts per minute in some cases. Given several hours or days, these dictionary tools will overcome any password. The secret is to make it as difficult as possible to crack your password.

Command and Control Server

Bots, Trojans and other malware typically are controlled by another off-network server called a Command and Control Server. This server accepts and collects information harvested by the individually infected computers or issues commands for the infected computers to perform such as Denial of Service Attacks. Some Command and Control Server can manage thousands or even hundreds of thousands computers that make up a Botnet.

Data Mining

Data mining is the automatic or semi-automatic analysis of large quantities of data to extract interesting patterns of data that can be used for various data analytics that can be used for marketing or other research. Companies like Google and Yahoo analyze information collected data from various sources including g-mail incoming and outgoing email, browsing activity, search engine results and other sources and then remarket the analytics collected to third parties.

Other similar terms are also used such as data dredging, data fishing, and data snooping and may be used interchangeably in many circles.

Not all data mining is bad. This term requires context. By now everyone has hear the term Bid Data. When it comes to Big Data, data mining is the process of sorting through HUGE data stock piles gathered from even bigger data sources for the purposes of providing research for marketing, trend analysis and a host of other legitimate pursuits. In this book we're using in the context of inappropriate or illegal gathering of confidential information without permission.

Encryption

Encryption is the process of encoding messages or information in such a way that only authorized parties can read it. Encryption doesn't prevent hacking but it reduces the likelihood that the hacker will be able to read the data that is encrypted. There a differing standards and levels of encryption. Commonly accepted types include: DES, 3DES, AES (128, 192, 256-bit)/MD5 and SHA-1. Each has a different level of complexity and sophistication.

Malware

Malware a contraction of the words Malicious and Software that defines any program, module or app that runs contrary to the desires of the owner of a computer, server or network device. It is also a broader definition of the more commonly used term – virus – which is actually a sub-category of Malware. The delineation is technical and is related to how the malware propagates itself. Simply put, viruses are designed to perpetuate copies of itself across multiple computers while most malware does not self-propagate once it infects a computer.

Network Sniffer (sniffing)

A network sniffer can monitor data flowing over computer network links. It can be a self-contained software program (or malware) or a hardware device with specially configured programming. Also sometimes called "network probes" or "snoops," sniffers examine network traffic, making a copy of the data but without redirecting or altering it. With that information, network traffic can be monitored and devices identified on your network.

Phishing

Phishing is the act of attempting to acquire sensitive information such as usernames, passwords, and credit card details (and sometimes, indirectly, money) by masquerading as a trustworthy entity in an electronic communication. Communications purporting to be from popular social web sites, auction sites, banks, online payment processors or IT administrators are commonly used to lure unsuspecting public. Phishing emails may contain links to websites that are infected with malware. Phishing is typically carried out by email spoofing or instant messaging, and it often directs users to enter details at a fake website whose look and feel are almost identical to the legitimate one. Phishing is an example of social engineering techniques used to deceive users, and exploits the poor usability of current web security technologies. Attempts to deal with the growing number of reported phishing incidents include legislation, user training, public awareness, and technical security measures.

RAT

A remote administration tool (a RAT) is a piece of software that allows a remote "operator" to control a system as if he has physical access to that system. While remote administration may have many legal uses, "RAT" software is usually associated with criminal or malicious activity. Malicious RAT software is typically installed without the victim's knowledge, often as payload of a Trojan horse, and will try to hide its operation from the victim and from security software.

Many Trojans and backdoors now have remote administration capabilities allowing a Hacker to control the victim's computer. These are generally sent through email, P2P file sharing software, and in internet downloads. They are usually disguised as a legitimate program or file. Many server files will display a fake error message when opened, to make it seem like it didn't open. Some RATs can also disable antivirus and firewall software.

Social Engineering

Social engineering is the modern con game: the hacker manipulates you to divulge your password or other confidential information by using some kind of convincing personal contact. This personal contact might involve direct face-to-face communications, like a pretty girl with a clipboard doing interviews in a shopping mall. Social engineering attacks might also occur over the phone, where a hacker will masquerade as a bank representative calling to confirm your phone number and bank account numbers. The third and by far the most common social engineering attack is called phishing or whaling via e-mail or pop-ups on the web. Phishing and whaling attacks can be deception pages masquerading as legitimate authorities on your computer screen. Phishing/whaling emails will often redirect the victim to a convincing phishing website masquerading as a well-known legitimate site, tricking the victim into typing in their personal account number and/or password, believing the website to be their actual bank or online account

Spoofing

Spoofing is a process where an intruder attempts to hide behind the identity of another intending to conceal their real identity, their location or to misdirect efforts to track the originator to track down the originator of improper activity. Spoofing e-mail addresses hides the identity of the original sender of spam and uses the sending address of some innocent third party. They accomplish this by stealing lists of legitimate e-mail accounts from insure address books or other sources and subsequently use of the stolen identities as the "spoofed" sender and the others as the targets of spam or malware.

Denial of Service (DOS or DDoS) attacks will frequently spoof the Internet IP address of legitimate organizations to mask the originating address of attacks to defeat efforts to stop the attacks or track back to the perpetrators.

The first technique is very easy to accomplish. The second requires a little more technical skill.

SSID

Wireless networks are identified by portable devices by a signal broadcast that is called an SSID. The SSID (Service Set Identifier) differentiates one WLAN (wireless local access network) from another, so all access points and all devices attempting to connect to a specific WLAN must use the same SSID to enable effective communication. SSIDs may be either broadcast or hidden depending upon the desired us. For example, if company A wants to provide internet access to staff to perform business functions while at work while at the same time provide public access to the Internet for guests, it can create a segment of the wireless network for non-public access (typically called a private wireless network SSID) and not broadcast an SSID for staff. It is known to employees only and no guest can even "see" the connection. Conversely, a public access SSID can be broadcast that can be detected by guest laptops or other portables for their use. The Guests are completely unaware of the private wireless access because it is undetectable. Prudent organizations still should require an access password for even public access to reduce the exposure their WLAN has to use of their connection for unauthorized or illegal purposes.

Bibliography

3 Advanced Threat Protection Essentials   By Paul Kaspian May 6, 2014 www.securityintelligence.com

Gartner: 'Five Styles of Advanced Threat Defense' can protect enterprise from targeted attacks" By Ellen Messmer, Network World October 30, 2013, www.networkworld.com

Gartner: "Gartner's 2013 Magic Quadrant Report for Unified Threat Management "- Jul 19, 2013   www.**gartner**.com

Gartner: "Gartners 2014 Magic Quadrant for Endpoint Protection Platform"s - January 8, 2014 Analyst(s): Peter Firstbrook, John Girard, Neil MacDonald   www.**gartner**.com

2012 Cost of Cyber Crime Study: United States - Ponemon Institute - http://www.ponemon.org

EssentiaLink - Business Continuity – Statistics & Industry Trends in 2013
http://essentialink.com/business-continuity-statistics-industry-trends-in-2013/

C/Net Article – "Google filing says Gmail users have no expectation of privacy"
by Steven Musil - C/Net August 13, 2013

About the Author

Jeff Hoffman

Jeff Hoffman is president of Applied Computer Technologies of Illinois, Inc. This 26 year old Managed Services and network support company has served the health services, government and non-profit industries in the northern Illinois area since 1988.

He holds a BA from National Louis University and has served in various management and technical positions in the IT industry for ACT and several Fortune 500 companies since 1971. He began his IT career as a mainframe programmer for Kemper Insurance in 1971. Mr. Hoffman served as the Project Manager/Lead Technologist for employee benefits activities for Baxter Healthcare International prior to founding ACT.

As Automation Systems Manager for Employee Benefits at Motorola, Inc. , Mr. Hoffman directed the IT activities of all employee insurance, benefits and compensation related activities for the world-wide Motorola organization of over 100,000 employees. He also served as a board member on the Minority Job Training Programs Advisory Council at Harry S. Truman College in Chicago.

As co-founder and Vice President of Operations, Mr. Hoffman also directed the development of Holland-America Systems as a leading importer and supplier to companies like Sears Roebuck, Bloomingdales and Tru-Value.

In 1988, Mr. Hoffman founded Applied Computer Technologies with his wife Deborah and has remained its president since that time. In 1991, ACT began concentrating on networking and security services for schools, corporate, non-profit and healthcare organizations.